THE MUSIC OF SILENCE

Blessed Elizabeth of the Trinity for Everyone

For Camilla and Angela
who both love Elizabeth

THE MUSIC OF SILENCE

Blessed Elizabeth of the Trinity for Everyone

Simplified and illustrated by
Elizabeth Ruth Obbard

New City

First published in 2016
in Great Britain by
New City

© 2016 Elizabeth Ruth Obbard

© Illustrated by Elizabeth Ruth Obbard

Graphic editor Sandy Bartus

British Cataloguing-in-Publication Data:
A catalogue record for this book is available from the
British Library

ISBN 978-1-905039-28-9

Typeset in Great Britain by
New City, London

Printed and bound by Gutenberg Press Ltd

CONTENTS

ELIZABETH AND JEANETTE

'ELIZABETH IS TEACHING HER DOLL
TO PRAY' (MADAME CATEZ)

INTRODUCING ELIZABETH

Early life

Elizabeth of the Trinity, Elizabeth Catez, was born on Sunday July 18th, 1880, and baptized on the feast of St Mary Magdalene (July 22nd). Seeing in all aspects of her life the hand of Divine Providence, Elizabeth saw God's Providence also at work in these simple facts, in that Sunday, the Lord's day, was the day of the Trinity for her, and Mary Magdalene was the saint of passionate love for the Master.

Elizabeth's mother, Marie Rolland, was the daughter of a good middle class family, her father being a retired Commandant and tax collector. Elizabeth's father, Joseph Catez, came from very poor antecedents in Northern France. The determination with which he pursued his career as a military man can be seen in that he rose through the ranks to become an officer, attaining the rank of Captain. The fact that he delayed marriage until he was commissioned and could take a bride that fitted his new status, is indicative of the drive and single mindedness he passed on to his elder daughter.

Elizabeth was the first child of the marriage and it was a difficult birth. Her mother was almost thirty four at the time and her father forty-eight; so her parents were no longer young and were already scarred by life's vicissitudes. For them she was a harbinger of joy and delight, a true miracle.

Elizabeth (nicknamed Sabeth) was a beautiful, lively child with a fierce temper and a strong will. When she was only nineteen months old her doll, Jeanette, was borrowed without her knowledge to be dressed as the child Jesus and placed in the crib at a service for the blessing of children. It was thought that in an embroidered robe the doll would not be recognised by her owner. But no! Elizabeth saw through the disguise immediately. She leapt up, her eyes bright with rage. 'Jeanette, give me back my Jeanette' she shouted. Her nurse had to carry her out to the general amusement of the congregation. Photographs of Elizabeth at this time show her with a strong pout beneath the beautiful dark eyes that soon became her most attractive feature.

Elizabeth grew up to the sound of military music and the life of the camp in which she lived at Bourges. Two and a half years later she would be joined by a sister, Marguerite (known as Guite.) The sisters were inseparable, and remained 'best friends' through all their growing years. However, tragedy struck the little family when Elizabeth was seven. One Sunday morning the recently retired Captain was struck down by a sudden heart attack and died in his daughter's arms.

As a widow on a modest military pension, Madame Catez and her two girls (hencefore designating themselves as 'The Trio') moved to Dijon where they took an apartment overlooking the garden of the nearby Carmel. In

MAMA

THE TRIO

SABETH   GUITE

Dijon Elizabeth began to see how her choleric temperament was causing her mother grief, and she resolved to overcome her sudden rages. So well did she succeed, that those who knew her only in later life, marvelling at her self-control and graciousness, thought that it came naturally.

Spiritual milestones

Elizabeth's First Confession, First Communion and Confirmation were all significant events in her young life. At her First Confession she made a strong resolve to conquer her temper, for she saw how her erratic moods pained her mother, whom she loved passionately. Her First Communion was the occasion of encountering more fully the Jesus she already longed for, a day on which she was supremely happy. 'I am no longer hungry, Jesus has fed me,' she confided to a friend, Marie Louise Hallo. Afterwards the children were invited to go to the Carmel and meet the prioress. Elizabeth joined the group, and the prioress, Mother Mary of Jesus, told her that her name meant 'House of God'. For Elizabeth this was another pointer towards her future vocation. She realised God dwelt within her and she should be there with him.

Meanwhile Madame Catez and her daughters continued to live as a social unit with many friends and acquaintances (although notably none of her father's family were included). Madame Catez loved to travel and the summer would see the little family going off by train to visit relatives in the South of France and elsewhere. Both Elizabeth and Marguerite showed exceptional musical talent and attended classes at the Dijon Conservatory. At home there was a governess for general education, but Elizabeth never mastered such things as spelling; she was too busy at the piano, where her talent was remarked on at the various concerts given by the Conservatory pupils. Each day saw her practising for hours. Her whole soul was attuned to music and it was a metaphor she often used in her later spiritual writings. When visiting friends Elizabeth was often called to the piano for duets. She could read music on sight and so was a much desired asset at parties and soirees.

However, beneath the social round and her ongoing development as a young woman, Elizabeth was growing in another direction – God was becoming the focus of her love and her life. Her First Communion had awakened a deep desire to give her Master love for love. Just before her fourteenth birthday she felt an irresistible urge to vow her virginity to God after Communion. Shortly afterwards the word 'Carmel' entered her soul, and the vocation to a life of prayer as lived in that Order became an irresistible attraction. When could she join the silent nuns she could see from her balcony as they walked in their enclosure garden?

The thought of a Carmelite vocation for her elder daughter was not a happy one for Madame Catez. She wanted to see her two girls well married and she forbade Elizabeth to visit the Carmel for a while, saying she would only countenance her entry at the age of twenty one, not before.

'I AM PLAYING A LOT OF MUSIC HERE'
(LETTER II)

The young woman

So Elizabeth, with her single mindedness, made the resolution to live with God in secular life with the same intensity as she might find in the cloister. God was with her always, she must be with him in the depths of her soul. It was in the years between seventeen and twenty-one that Elizabeth realised that living with God could be practised in the midst of many varied occupations. Friendliness and gaiety marked her dealings with everyone. She was no solemn killjoy, but the picture of elegance, herself and Guite sporting the latest fashions in dresses and hats. People loved her, and she was never to cease encouraging her correspondents, when she herself was in Carmel, to find God within themselves even in the midst of busy lives. In her private notes during this time she wrote:

For my heart is always with Him.
Day and night it thinks unceasingly
Of its heavenly and divine Friend.

Meanwhile Elizabeth continued her social engagements, received a very advantageous offer of marriage (which, much to her mother's disappointment, she refused), ate enormous meals when visiting friends on holiday: 'They gave us such enormous meals our stomachs were begging for mercy,' she wrote amusingly. She travelled, played music, danced, helped out in the parish with catechising children, socialised with girls of her own age and class;

but on another level her heart was elsewhere. Those dark eyes of hers became pools harbouring an inner light. They reflected a growing attachment to Carmel and a desire to give herself radically to God alone. And so the time passed...

As her twenty first birthday approached Madame Catez tried to put off the hour of Elizabeth's entrance, but Elizabeth stood firm, even though she knew the grief that parting would cause her mother and sister. It was a real trial of faith. Elizabeth had been given permission to visit the Carmel once more and she struck up a friendship with the prioress and with other young girls considering a vocation. In fact the Carmel of Dijon had so many new young aspirants that a foundation was about to be made at Paray-le-Monial. Mother Mary of Jesus wanted Elizabeth to enter there and her trunks had already been sent ahead. But then the prioress saw the additional agony it caused Madame Catez to think of her daughter far away in another city, and she relented. Elizabeth would enter Dijon after all. It was an inspired decision in that Elizabeth was the kind of person who needed a regular and settled religious life, not all the activity and upheaval of a new foundation.

Elizabeth's entry date was set for August 2nd, a first Friday and, for Franciscans, the feast of the dedication of the Church of St Mary of the Angels, the Portiuncula, a fitting feast for one who knew herself to be a 'House of God'.

Before leaving home for the last time Elizabeth knelt before the portrait of her father and asked for his blessing. Then, after morning Mass, with her mother and sister beside her, she passed through the door of Carmel's enclosure. The life she had wanted and longed for was now hers.

Life in Carmel

Carmelite life is basically a life of prayer, a life of 'hermits living in community' after the example of those first hermits who settled on Mount Carmel in Northern Israel during the time of the Crusades. The great Saint Teresa of Avila had adapted this life for women living within strict enclosure. In Elizabeth's time the timetable included two hours of silent prayer a day, the full Divine Office, a period for spiritual reading and other periods of silence and solitude in the cell. Every Sunday the Blessed Sacrament was exposed in the oratory and Elizabeth would kneel there for long hours.

Then there was the work that is part of all community living. Elizabeth was extremely happy in those early days. Everything delighted her. She was with a fervent group of sisters and she revelled in helping with the wash, the plain sewing, the hours of recreation, the daily routine which supported her in her love of interior recollection. Her official name, Mary Elizabeth of the Trinity, seemed a felicitous choice on the part of the prioress, and it became another impetus to living with the Trinitarian God within. Such happiness convinced Elizabeth she was in the right place. She glowed with good health and put on weight. During those first months she wrote to her family:

> *To eat well, to sleep well, they say, are the conditions for making a good Carmelite: in that I leave nothing to be desired. (Letter 94)*

On December 8th, feast of the Immaculate Conception, which fell on a Sunday that year, Elizabeth received her longed for Carmelite habit. Entering the Church wearing a beautiful white satin wedding dress her family and friends said her joy was ecstatic.

Shortly afterwards, on Christmas Day of that year, 1901, she wrote in her notes:

> *Silence is my joy.*
> *I listen to Him in peace,*
> *His presence close.*
> *To Him I surrender myself.*
> *Spotless, meek Lamb,*
> *You are everything to me.*
> *You know how I hunger*
> *To be entirely Yours.*
> *Your betrothed desires*
> *To feed on You,*
> *To be consumed by You,*
> *Surrendered completely.*

I want to be Yours,
Living for You alone,
Your living Host,
Consumed by You on the Cross.

Novitiate

In her new habit Elizabeth looked forward to deepening her knowledge of religious life and growing in the love of God. Up until now that life had pleased her in every respect, but suddenly darkness descended on her spirit. She had to struggle to go to prayer, to be faithful, to continue along the way on which she had set out. Her prioress and sisters noticed the strain she was labouring under, but realised that everyone has to undergo periods of trial and painful self-knowledge. In her correspondence Elizabeth gave no hint of her troubles. She encouraged others to live in trust and self-forgetfulness as she herself was having to do.

As for the source of her trials, it may have been the tender attachment she felt for her young prioress, Mother Germaine (who was also the novice mistress), that needed to be purified. Additionally she was having to live without the music that had sustained and lifted her spirits for so many years. Carmelites did not sing the Office. They preserved a very austere liturgical tradition and there was singing only at recreation, and that without any instrumental accompaniment. Occasionally on a

A CARMELITE IS ONE WHO HAS GAZED ON THE CRUCIFIED (LETTER 133)

HE IS MY ONE AND ALL

big feast Marguerite would arrange for musicians to come and play during Benediction but that was all. For a young woman, whose life and soul had breathed music, it must have been a real deprivation to go without it in practice, even if in theory one had generously offered the sacrifice in advance. The cold, the lack of social interaction with her many friends, the proximity of her mother and sister still grieving her absence, the bleakness of her prayer when she had, as she said, to force herself to remain before the Blessed Sacrament on Sundays when she longed to be elsewhere, all combined to add to her loneliness and sense of alienation.

Yet at this time Elizabeth could write to a friend:

The life of a Carmelite is a communion with God from morning to evening, and from evening to morning. If He did not fill our cells and cloisters, ah, how empty they would be! But through everything we see Him, for we bear Him within us, and our life is an anticipated heaven. I ask God to teach you all these secrets. (Letter 123)

These were secrets that Elizabeth herself had to learn. God dwelt within her as she well knew and had known for years. It was for her to be with him in faith, not feeling.

A Carmelite is a soul who has gazed on the Crucified One; who has seen Him offering Himself as a Victim to His Father for souls... has understood the passionate love of His soul and wanted to give herself as He did! On the mountain of Carmel in silence and solitude, in a prayer that never ends – for it continues through everything – the Carmelite already lives with God alone as in heaven... She finds Him everywhere; through everything she sees His radiance! Is this not heaven on earth! (Letter 133)

Elizabeth knew that what was offered to her in her own vocation was offered to every baptised person. Every Christian is a temple of the Spirit, a house of God, called to live in faith, called to a life infused with prayer and the presence of God who dwells in us. If Elizabeth had seemed to live always in the light she could not be a model for those of us who walk in dark faith.

That year she was to write in her personal notes:

The Carmelite is a given soul,
on fire with love for the glory of God.
She is crucified with Christ,
but her Calvary is radiant with light.
Gazing on Him her soul is set ablaze.
She understood His calling and exclaimed
'Here I am', my heart is wounded, yet given to You.

The Carmelite is an adoring soul,
surrendered to God's action within her,
communing with God whatever comes,
her heart and her eyes fixed on heaven alone.
Only one thing is necessary and she has found it,
the Divine Being who is Light and Love.

She enfolds the world in her prayer,
as a true apostle.

The novitiate year was ending and Elizabeth was received for Profession, the date being set for Sunday January 11th, that year the feast of the Epiphany. Some days beforehand she went to join her mother and sister outside the cloister for her canonical examination, when a priest came to ascertain that she was seeking this commitment of her own free will. Photographs of the occasion were taken by Georges Chevignard who had married Marguerite two months earlier. Elizabeth looks strained, and indeed on the very eve of Profession a priest had to be sent for to assure the worried nun that she was indeed called to Carmelite life by God.

After making her vows all doubts fled. Elizabeth knew a peace that surpassed understanding. Receiving her profession crucifix she knew she was now all his, and FOREVER.

Towards death

Elizabeth's life continued to unfold as she developed an understanding of her personal vocation. She knew herself as Elizabeth of the Trinity:

I am 'Elizabeth of the Trinity,' that is, Elizabeth
disappearing, losing herself, letting herself be possessed by
the Three. (Letter 172)

Later she was to choose another name for herself, 'Laudem Gloriae' the 'Praise of Glory'. Immersed in the writings of her beloved St Paul she studied his epistles and pondered them assiduously. For her, life's only meaning began to be a simple act of praise, of self-forgetfulness, of decreasing so that the life of Christ the Master might come to full flowering in her, and she become for him 'another humanity in which he could renew all his mystery'. (Prayer to the Trinity)

She was still young but, unbeknown to her, death was not far away. She felt a growing lassitude, lack of energy, inability to digest her food. Addison's disease had already taken over her body and at this time was incurable. Gradually Elizabeth lost weight until she looked like a skeleton. Her tongue felt as if it were on fire. She dragged herself to the tribune of the chapel and huddled there seeking to pray even in the midst of her pain.

Elizabeth then began to write to her friends and family (her mother, sister and brother-in-law already knew of her approaching death) to say goodbye. She wanted, she said, to leave them her legacy of loving the Triune God within so that they too could become 'Praises of Glory'.

To her prioress, Mother Germaine, whom she loved with special affection, she wrote her last testament, exhorting her to 'let herself be loved'. This phrase is typical of Elizabeth. Letting ourselves be loved is to surrender to all God asks with a trusting, childlike heart. Jesus asked Peter 'Do you love me?' We may want to respond with our 'Yes, we love you Lord,' but the more important question

LET yourself

be LOVED

is, do we allow God to love us? For Elizabeth that meant in her illness being transformed into the Crucified Christ, bearing in her own body all that had to be made up for the sake of Christ's body, the Church, becoming incarnate love for others. She revered Mother Germaine as a priest, deputed to offer God the soul and body of the dying nun as the priest offers the Body of Christ at Mass, transforming the bread and wine into the body and blood of the Son of God. For this Mother Germaine must 'let herself be loved' above all others, so that she can fulfil her priestly role with the utmost dedication. Elizabeth could not do it alone. She needed her spiritual mother for this important office. Mother Germaine must 'let herself be loved' as Elizabeth was 'letting' God love her in her pain and diminishment.

Towards the end of her life Elizabeth wrote two retreats, one for herself and one for her sister. They have been chosen and slightly adapted to help the reader savour Elizabeth's teaching, and her invitation to a life of deep prayer. The themes are self-explanatory and she repeats them in various guises: self-forgetfulness, the primacy of faith, persevering in prayer, abiding in peace even in the midst of the trials of daily life.

The other text is her famous prayer to the Trinity. With these everyone can be led into Elizabeth's silence, and share her secret of total surrender in love to the One she called her 'Three'.

The Scripture quotations are from the RSV, apart from a few where a freer translation was necessary.

PRAYER TO THE TRINITY

On November 21st 1904, the feast of the Presentation of the child Mary in the temple, the Dijon community renewed their vows of religious profession. The Presentation of Mary is a feast with a long history, originating in the Eastern Church and based on a legend found in the apocryphal Gospel of James. It states that at the age of three Mary's parents took her to the temple where she was to be brought up and educated in its sacred precincts. Filled with joy at being in God's house she ran up the temple steps to the waiting high priest. There is no historical foundation for this feast, but in the East it is often known as the feast of the 'Silence of Mary', commemorating the fact that Mary was prepared in silence and prayer from her earliest years for the mission that still lay ahead as mother of God's son.

It seems that after renewing her vows Elizabeth felt an irresistible movement of love for the Trinity. When she returned to her cell she penned the following prayer on a sheet of paper torn from a notebook without a single correction. It was found in her papers after her death.

As a prayer it summarises Elizabeth's main themes: adoration, silence, peace, conformity to Christ, surrender to the Holy Spirit. So all-encompassing is this prayer that it has found its way into the Catechism of the Catholic Church.

Prayer

O my God, Trinity whom I adore,
let me entirely forget myself,
that I may abide in you,
still and peaceful
as if my soul were already in eternity.
Let nothing disturb my peace,
nor separate me from you, my unchanging God.
May each moment take me further
into the depths of your mystery!

Establish my soul in peace!
Make it your heaven,
your cherished abode,
the place of your rest.
May I never abandon you there,
but may I be ever attentive,
ever alert in my faith,
ever adoring and all given up
to your creative action.

O my beloved Christ, crucified for love,
would that I might be for you a spouse of your heart!
I would anoint you with glory,

I would love you – even unto death!
Yet I sense my frailty
and ask you to adorn me with yourself,
to identify my soul with all the movements of your soul.
Immerse me in yourself.
Possess me completely.
Substitute yourself for me,
that my life may be but a reflection of your life.
Come into me as Adorer, Redeemer and Saviour!

O Eternal Word, Word of my God,
Would that I might spend my life listening to you,
would that I might be fully receptive to learn all from you.
Then through all darkness, all loneliness, all weakness,
may I ever keep my eyes fixed on you
and abide under your great light.
O my beloved star, hold me in such a way
that I may never be able to leave your radiance!

O consuming fire, Spirit of Love!
Descend into my soul
and make all in me as an incarnation of the Word,
that I may be to him another humanity
in which he can renew all his mystery.

And you, O Father,
bend down to your poor little creature,
seeing in her none other than your beloved Son
in whom you are well pleased.

O my 'Three', my all, my beatitude,
infinite solitude, immensity in whom I lose myself,
I give myself to you as a prey to be consumed.
Bury yourself in me
that I may bury myself in you,
until I depart to contemplate in your light
the abyss of your greatness!

ESTABLISH MY SOUL IN PEACE

GUITE & FAMILY

'GOD LOVES YOU, MY GUITE: YOUR UNION IS
WHOLLY BLESSED BY HIM! YOU WILL SEE THAT
BOTH OF US ARE BLESSED IN OUR OWN WAY.'
(LETTER 140)

RETREAT FOR HER SISTER
'HEAVEN ON EARTH'

Elizabeth wrote the following retreat as a present for her sister Marguerite (Guite) who had asked her for some guidance on living an interior life. At the time of writing Elizabeth had only a few months to live and Guite received the manuscript after her sister's death.

At this time Guite (aged 22) was married to Georges Chevignard and they had two small daughters. They would go on to have nine children, of whom several entered the priesthood or religious life. Guite's eldest daughter, another Elizabeth, later joined the Carmel of Dijon.

Guite and Elizabeth were exceptionally close, and she and Elizabeth nearly always dressed alike as children and young women. Their father's death had drawn the mother and her daughters closer together and they thought of themselves as 'The Trio'. Elizabeth's entry into Carmel was a real grief to the family as it broke up what had seemed to be an inseparable unit.

Elizabeth had hoped that Guite would one day join the Dijon Carmel too, but at the age of nineteen, not long after Elizabeth's entry, Guite fell in love with Georges

Chevignard, a banker and fellow musician. They married on the feast of St Teresa in order to unite themselves in spirit with the Carmelite sisters who were celebrating the feast of their foundress on the same day, October 15th.

When the children were born Elizabeth became a devoted aunt and was overjoyed when the couple named their first child, a daughter, after her, nicknaming her Sabeth, Elizabeth's own childhood diminutive.

Although Guite was now a banker's wife and a busy mother, Elizabeth was quick to assure her that she too was called to live with the indwelling God. Through her relationship with Guite, Elizabeth found herself growing in the understanding of what it meant to be God's child. She writes:

I have just been reading in St Paul some splendid things on the mystery of divine adoption.
Naturally I thought of you – it would have been quite extraordinary if I hadn't: you who are a mother and who know what depths of love God has placed in your heart for your children, you can grasp the grandeur of this mystery. To be children of God, my Guite, doesn't that thrill you? Through everything, in the midst of your maternal cares, while you give yourself to your little angels, you can retire into the house of our Father, in 'the centre of our souls', in order to surrender yourself to the Holy Spirit, so that He may transform you in God, and imprint on your soul the

Image of the divine Beauty; so that the Father, lovingly bending over you, may see only His Christ. (Letter 239)

Seeing Guite maturing as a mother and wife, Elizabeth understood in a deeper way that we are all called to love and be loved no matter what vocation we may follow. The heart of a mother is a reflection of the very heart of God. As Guite and Georges loved their children, so God loves us without condition and without reserve.

To her little nieces (Elizabeth only lived long enough to see Guite's first two children) she left a letter telling them that they too were destined, through Baptism, to be conformed to the image of Jesus: 'He has clothed you with himself, thus making you his children, and at the same time his living temples.' Little Sabeth and her sister Odette reminded her of herself and Guite as children. She saw in the elder one the same protective love she herself had felt for the young Guite in being her 'big sister'. Looking at them in the light of faith she sees them as being carried in the arms of God from all eternity. They may look small but their destiny is great. Elizabeth had a true reverence for the mystery of the person – unique and unrepeatable in each one – yet each called to reflect Christ in the world in a new and beautiful way.

This retreat for Guite was written in the form of consecutive prayers. Of course, a mother could not just abandon her responsibilities, but she could at least carve out a few minutes to ponder on her Christian calling and God's desire for her to surrender herself to him completely. As always Elizabeth relies heavily on Scripture, which, after all, was not written for nuns and priests, but for all who share a common Baptism, even if lived out in varying ways.

The passages given here have been somewhat shortened in order to highlight one particular theme for each day.

PRAYER 1
Living with God

Father, I desire that they also, whom you have given me, may be with me where I am, to behold my glory which you have given me in your love for me before the foundation of the world. (Jn 17: 24)

These words show us Christ's last desire.
They are his prayer before he returns to the Father.
He wills that where he is we may be too,
not only in eternity but also in time,
for eternity has already begun for us here on earth.

Where then are we to be with him?
How can his ideal be realised?
St John of the Cross says
that the Son is hidden in the bosom of the Father,
hidden from our understanding and our vision.

Isaiah too says: 'Truly, you are a God who hides yourself, O God of Israel the Saviour.' (Is. 45: 15)

Yet it is Christ's will that we abide permanently in him. That we should dwell where he dwells in the unity of love, that we should be, so to speak, God's shadow.

Yes, the Blessed Trinity is our dwelling place. Our true home is our Father's house which we should never leave.

WELCOME HOME

PRAYER 2
Abide in me

Abide in me and I in you. (Jn 14: 4)

This command is given and this desire expressed by the very Word of God.

'Abide in me', not just for a few moments, not even for a few passing hours. Rather, abide in me permanently and habitually.

Abide in me.
Pray in me.
Adore in me.
Love in me.
Suffer in me.
Work in me.
Act in me.
Whatever you are doing, whatever concerns you,
keep penetrating deeper into this place of abiding.

However, to really listen (and not just listen superficially) we must immerse ourselves ever more deeply in God. We must descend daily into the depths of God with loving confidence and trust.

'Deep calls to deep' (Ps. 42: 7),
and when we sink into the depths of our nothingness
we will find ourselves face to face

with the infinite depths of God's mercy.
There we will discover the strength to die to self
and be transformed in love.
'Blessed are the dead who die in the Lord.' (Rev. 14: 13)

DEEP calls to DEEP

SINK INTO YOUR NOTHINGNESS

AND DISCOVER

MERCY

PRAYER 3
The kingdom within

The kingdom of God is within you. (Lk. 17: 21)

God has just invited us to abide in him
that we may live our heritage of glory.
We are not to go outside ourselves to find this treasure.
The kingdom is with us, among us and within us.

St John of the Cross says that the innermost core of the soul
is inaccessible to the world and the Evil One.
There God gives Godself to us.
Every movement of our soul then becomes divine.

The Lord effects this in us so that whatever we do is both
God's and ours.

When we love fully and comprehensively,
when we enjoy God with all our strength,
then we access our soul's deepest centre – God.
When we have not yet attained this point we may still be
in God but there is room left for us to advance deeper into
the Divine.

Love unites us to God, and the greater the love the more
deeply do we enter into God.
If we have only one degree of love we are already in God.
But when we have attained the highest degree of love we
will be transformed into God's own likeness.

PRAYER 4
Keeping God's word

*If any love me, they will keep my word, and my Father
will love them, and we will come and make our home with
them. (cf Jn 14: 23)*

Again we hear that the Master wants to dwell within us. 'If anyone loves me...' It is this which draws God to us. Real love is not an emotion. It is love 'strong as death... which many waters cannot quench, no floods drown'. (Song 8: 6-7)

Our Master says: 'I love the Father,' (Jn 14: 31)
and 'I always do what pleases him.' (Jn 8: 28)
Anyone who wants to keep close to Jesus
should live by his words.
The divine Will must be our daily bread.

THE DIVINE WILL

IS OUR

Daily Bread

We should allow ourselves to be wholly given over
to the Father's good pleasure, as was Christ crucified,
who is the object of our adoration.

Every occurrence,
every event,
every suffering,
every joy
is a sacrament which gives us God.

As we progress along this path we stop distinguishing
between the pleasant and the unpleasant, but pass through
everything that happens in order to rest in God alone.

Love holds nothing back but gives all to the beloved.
Happy are we when we love
because then God is held captive by our love.

PRAYER 5
Your life is hidden with Christ in God

You have died and your life is hidden with Christ in God.
(Col. 3: 3)

What does 'You have died' mean?
Surely it means that when we really want to live in God,
in the fortress of our inner selves,

FIX YOUR ATTENTION ON GOD

we must be detached in spirit
and withdrawn from the thought of everything else.

We need to develop in ourselves
a simple, loving tending towards God,
no matter what happens to us.

If we have this inner focus
then we are not affected by what passes
for we step over everything with our attention fixed on God.

This is to die daily to self
so that Christ may grow greater within us.

No matter what we feel, we can find joy in everything, for
it enables us to give place to the Master we love.

PRAYER 6
Our God is a consuming fire

Our God is a consuming fire. (Heb. 12: 29)

Our God is a fire of love which destroys, but also a fire
that transforms into itself whatever it touches.

Mystical death becomes very sweet and simple to those
who yield themselves up to the action of its flames
in the depths of their being.
Instead of thinking of the work of detachment and
destruction that they still have to accomplish,
they want only to plunge into the furnace of love
burning within them.

That furnace is the Holy Spirit, the bond of love
between the Father and the Son, the Word of God.

People abandoned to love's flames
enter into God through a living faith.

In simplicity and peace they are raised above
all feelings of devotion
and penetrate into the 'sacred darkness'
where they are transformed into the divine image.

They live in communion
with the three persons of the Trinity.
This is the contemplative life.

PRAYER 7
Casting fire upon earth

*I came to cast fire upon the earth; and would that it were
already kindled. (Lk. 12: 49)*

The Master himself tells us
that he wants to see the fire of love set ablaze.
Everything we do and work at are nothing in his sight.
We cannot give God anything,
nor can we ourselves satisfy God's one desire,
which is to enhance the dignity of our inner being.

God wants to see us growing in the divine likeness.
The gift of love is what puts lover and beloved on a par.
The one who possesses such love
appears in some way equal to Jesus,
because mutual love makes the lovers share everything in
common.

To attain this love
we must have surrendered ourselves entirely.
The will must be sweetly lost in God's will,
so that everything we do and say and think
may be moved in and by love alone.

Everything I do, I do in love.
Everything I suffer, I suffer in love.
This is what David means when he sings

'I will keep my strength for you.'
We are then so filled, absorbed and protected by love
that we find the secret of growing in love wherever we are.
Even in the midst of the world and the daily cares of life
we can truly say with St John of the Cross
that 'Love is my sole occupation.'

LOVERS SHARE EVERYTHING

PRAYER 8
We must believe

Whoever would draw near to God must believe. (Heb. 11: 6)
Faith is the assurance of things hoped for, the conviction of
things not seen. (Heb. 11: 1)

Faith is what makes future blessings
appear so certain, and so present to us,
that they exist for us as really as if we enjoyed them now.

St John of the Cross says the feet of faith take us to God.
So we should choose faith above all else, for faith fills us
with spiritual gifts and the knowledge of God.

When speaking to the Samaritan woman
Christ alluded to faith when he promised to give believers
'a fountain of water springing up into everlasting life'.
(Jn 4: 14)

'We have known and believed the love God has for us.'
(1 Jn 4: 16)
This is our great act of faith,
the means of giving God love for love.
It is the 'mystery hidden in the heart of the Father'
of which St Paul speaks. (cf Col. 1: 26)

Through faith we leap over all obstacles
to find rest in the heart of infinite Love.

TAKES US TO GOD

Faith does works of love,
and so we can hear the Master whisper to us
the words he once spoke to Mary Magdalene:
'Your faith has saved you. Go in peace.' (Lk. 7: 50)

PRAYER 9
Conformed to the image of the Son

*Those whom he foreknew he also destined to be conformed
to the image of his Son... Who then shall separate us from
the love of Christ? (Rom 8: 29, 35)*

Surely we are one of those foreknown, predestined and
elected. God can say to us as was said of old through the
prophet:
'When I passed by you again and looked at you, behold,
you were at the age for love. And I spread my skirt over

you and covered your nakedness: Yes, I plighted my troth
to you and entered into a covenant with you, says the
Lord God, and you became mine.' (Ez. 16: 8)

Yes, we have become God's by Baptism.
We have received the seal of the Blessed Trinity.
At the same time, in St Peter's words, we were
'made partakers of the divine nature.' (2 Pet. 1: 4)

LET US CONTEMPLATE THE SON

Then we were justified by the Sacraments,
touched by faith in the very centre of our soul.
And the more we cultivate faith
the more we enter into the redemptive work of Christ.

Finally God wills to glorify us, making us 'partakers of the
heritage of the saints in the light.' (Col. 1: 12)
But we shall be glorified in the measure that we have been
conformed to the image of the Son.

Let us contemplate the Son continually.
Let us stay within the radiance of this image
that it may be impressed upon us.
Then we will truly take on the mind of Christ.

PRAYER 10
For me to live is Christ

*Whatever gain I had I counted as loss for the sake of Christ.
Indeed, I count everything as loss because of the surpassing
worth of knowing Christ Jesus my Lord. (Phil. 3: 7-8)*

To become like Christ we must study him,
so as to be conformed to him.
We must be so wholly merged in him that we can say:
'I live, now not I, but Christ lives in me.
And the life I now live in the flesh

I live by faith in the Son of God
who loved me and gave himself for me.' (Gal. 2: 20)

On coming into the world Christ proclaimed
that he came only to do the will of the Father.
For thirty-three years this will was his daily bread,
until on the cross he could truly say
'It is consummated.' (Jn 19: 30)
Yes, ALL has been done according to the will of the
Father.

Of course, if it gets too painful we can ask, as Jesus did,
that if it be possible the chalice might pass us by,
but we will immediately add 'Your will, not mine, be done.'

In this way we too can ascend the hill of Calvary
with a song of thanksgiving on our lips.
This will conform us to Jesus,
the image that the Father has wanted to imprint on our
souls before the beginning of time.

PRAYER 11
Adopted as God's children

He destined us in love
to be his adopted children through Jesus Christ,
according to the purpose of his will,
to the praise of his glorious grace,
which he freely bestowed on us in the beloved.' (Eph. 1: 5-6)

If we are truly children of God
we are moved and led by the Spirit of God,
and can cry out with Jesus, 'Abba, Father'.

We pray to our Father in heaven,
but we must seek the Father above all
in the heaven he has made for himself
in the very centre of our hearts.

Christ told the Samaritan woman that the Father
seeks adorers in spirit and in truth. (cf Jn 6:23)
Let us be such true adorers and so give God joy.

Let us fill our minds with God
in the knowledge imparted by faith.
Let us adore in truth by the way we act,
doing always what pleases the Father,
whose children we are.

Let us adore in Christ and with Christ,
for he alone is the true adorer.
If we really surrender, we shall learn by experience
the truth that Isaiah speaks of when he says;
'You shall be carried at the breasts and fondled on the
knees.' (Is. 66: 12)

Listen to this mysterious invitation:
'My child, give me your heart.' (Prov. 23: 26)

PRAYER 12
Living with Mary

There is one created being who knew the gift of God,
a creature who did not lose a particle of that gift;
a creature so pure and luminous
that she seemed to be the Light itself.
She is the faithful virgin
who 'kept all these things in her heart'. (Lk. 2: 51)
Mary was so lowly, so hidden in God,
that she drew down upon herself the loving gaze of the
Trinity:
'He has regarded the humility of his handmaiden,
for behold, from henceforth,
all generations will call me blessed.' (Lk. 1: 48)

The Father, bending over this woman so unaware of her
own beauty, chose her to be the mother of his Son.
Then the Spirit of Love overshadowed her
and, at her consent, the greatest of all mysteries took
place: she received the Word in her womb.
Mary thus became God's own forever.

During the period between the Annunciation and the
Nativity, Our Lady seems to me to be the model of all
those whom God calls to live contemplatively.

Mary lived and acted in such peace and recollection
that whatever she was doing, even the most trivial thing,

was made holy by her constant adoration of God within.

Yet, that did not prevent her from spending herself for others. The Gospel tells us that 'Mary arose and went with haste into the hill country, to a city of Judah' (Lk. 1: 39) to visit her cousin Elizabeth.
The reality she contemplated within herself
did not lesson her charity towards others,
for true prayer leads us to others even while we possess God.

PRAYER 13
Becoming a 'Praise of Glory'

We who first hoped in Christ have been destined to live for the praise of his glory. (Eph. 1: 12)

How can we fulfil this dream of the heart of God? How can we become perfect 'praises of his glory' the glory of the Blessed Trinity?

A 'Praise of Glory' is a person who dwells in God.
She lives for God with a pure, disinterested love.
She does not seek self and sweetness.
She loves God above all God's gifts.
She does not love according to gifts received
but desires only the good pleasure of God.

She does God's will, which ordains all things well.

A 'Praise of Glory' is silent,
so her instrument reverberates
at the slightest touch of the Holy Spirit,
who can draw forth divine harmonies from it.
Suffering produces an exquisite musical tone
which sweetly moves the heart of God
and gives joy to the musician.

A 'Praise of Glory' is one
who contemplates God in faith and simplicity.
She becomes an abyss into which God can flow,
a crystal through which God can shine,
and see the reflection of the divine splendour.
A 'Praise of Glory' is one with whom God can communicate
all God is and has.

Lastly, a 'Praise of Glory' is one
who is always giving thanks.
Her thoughts, actions, hopes, desires,
while ever establishing her more deeply in love,
are like an echo of the eternal 'Sanctus'.

One day the veil will be drawn back
and we shall be brought into the eternal courts of heaven.
There we shall sing in the heart of infinite Love.
There God will give us 'the new name'
promised to the one who overcomes. (Rev. 4: 8,10)

What will that name be?
It will be 'Laudem Gloriae' the 'Praise of Glory'. (Eph. 1: 12)

LAUDEM GLORIAE · A PRAISE OF GLORY

LAST RETREAT

On August 2nd 1906 Elizabeth celebrated the fifth anniversay of her entrance into Carmel, for her an unforgettable day which heralded her longed for commitment to a life of intense prayer and surrender to the Master she so loved. Her body, weakened and exhausted by Addison's disease, longing for rest yet unable to sleep, Elizabeth settled herself by the window of the infirmary and looked out over the dark and silent cloisters. Her heart was filled with a deep peace, and a true gratitude for all that those five years had meant to her. But she also knew that she would not see this anniversary again. Death, and the thought of death, were her constant companions.

Two weeks later, on August 15th, Elizabeth asked Mother Germaine if she could go into retreat. She knew well that the end was near, indeed she would not even live another three months. As the disease made inroads on her physical being, causing intense pain, vomiting, blinding headaches and an inability to eat or digest food, so her longing for consummating the sacrifice of her life grew. This retreat would be the prelude to eternity.

Her body weakened yet her spirit seemed to draw strength

from a divine source. She had already chosen her new name of 'Laudem Gloriae', the 'Praise of Glory'. Now she wanted to spend the time left to her on earth preparing to sing the praises of the Trinity in heaven. Over the past months she had gradually learned to forget herself completely, as she had prayed in her celebrated prayer to the Trinity, in order that God could have full scope in her life.

Elizabeth saw this retreat then as her 'novitiate' for heaven. There she would receive, not the Carmelite habit, but the raiment of glory that would conform her completely to Christ crucified. During this retreat she would spend every ounce of energy reliving her first Clothing Ceremony. The day when she had received the habit of Carmel was for her a day of intense, almost ecstatic joy, as her visitors said when they saw her radiant expression. So now she forced herself to make the same prostrations once again. She had been clothed on the feast of Mary's Immaculate Conception, now she hoped Mary would clothe her soon with the fine linen worn by the Bride of the Lamb.

Calling on Mother Germaine to be her 'priest' and offer Elizabeth to the Father as a victim is offered on the altar, Elizabeth entered her time of retreat as one leaving to others the legacy of her faith, her understanding of what it meant to live for the praise of God's glory in the depths of her being. She would spend the time with the statue of Our Lady of Lourdes beside her. This statue, which she had brought into Carmel with her, she named 'Janua Coeli', gate of heaven. The last photo of Elizabeth shows her skeletal frame with 'Janua Coeli' on the table beside her. Standing alone Mary symbolises the silent, recollected woman with whom Elizabeth identified, wholly intent on the God she bears within her.

As always, in this retreat Elizabeth relies heavily on the writings of her beloved St Paul. Indeed many of the meditations are almost a string of successive quotes from his letters. But she also hones in on the Book of Revelation in which she sees glimpses into the life of the heaven she is preparing to enter.

As before, the originial text has been slightly altered.

DAY 1
Knowing nothing but him

Nescivi – I know not. So sings the bride of the Spiritual Canticle after having been brought into the inner wine cellar:

All they who serve are telling me
of your unnumbered graces;
and all wound me more and more;
and something leaves me dying, I know not what – *nescivi* –
of which they are darkly speaking. (John of the Cross SC 7)

Nescivi – I know not.
It seems to me that this should also be
the song of a 'Praise of Glory'.

Nescivi – I know nothing, I desire to know nothing
but 'him… that I may may share his sufferings,
becoming like him in his death.' (Phil. 3: 10)
'Those whom he foreknew he also predestined
to be conformed to the image of his Son' (Rom 8: 10),
who was crucified for love.
When I have become identified completely with this Son,
dwelling always in him and he in me,
I shall fulfil my true vocation.
It is a calling chosen for me by God from the beginning,
and which I shall live out in eternity.

No one has penetrated the depths of Christ
as did Our Lady.
St John and St Mary Magdalene journeyed far into it,
and St Paul often speaks of the knowledge he himself
has received of it.
Yet all the saints dwell in shadow
compared to the light that was Our Lady's light!
She kept the secret in her heart
and pondered it unceasingly.
No tongue can tell of it, no pen express it.

This Mother of grace will so shape my soul
that I, who am her little child,
may become a living image of her 'firstborn',
the Son of the Eternal Father, the Father's perfect praise.

DAY 2
In silence

My soul is continually in my hands. (Ps. 118: 109)

This was the song of my Master's soul,
the reason why, even in the midst of anguish,
he remained calm and strong.

'My soul is continually in my hands.' What does this mean
except perfect self-control in the presence of the God of
peace.

'I will keep my strength for you.' (Ps 58: 10)
This is another of Christ's songs
in which I desire to participate continually.
My Rule (the Rule of St Albert followed by all Carmelites)
tells me that 'Your strength will lie in silence and hope.'
To keep our strength for the Lord
is to keep our whole being silent.
It is to collect all our powers
and occupy them in the one work of love.
It is to have the 'single eye'
which allows God's light to show us the way we should go.

How necessary it is to have unity of soul
if we want to live the life of the spirit,
for spirits are simple, uncomplicated beings.
Christ spoke to Magdalene of the 'one thing necessary'.
(Lk. 10: 42)
And how well Magdalene, this great saint,
recognised her God by faith under the veil of his
humanity.

Nescivi. Yes! She knows nothing but him.
Nescivi – no matter what noise and bustle might be
around her.
Nescivi – she might be blamed. So what?

Neither care for her honour, nor any outward thing
could draw Magdalene from her sacred silence.

This is what it is like for us
when we dwell in the fortress of holy recollection.
By the light of faith we see God present,
dwelling within us.
And we are present to God in a simplicity
that God guards with jealous care.

Then whatever happens to us without or within: *Nescivi.*
God may hide or withdraw loving feelings: *Nescivi.*
From now on the Master is supremely free to give himself
'according to the measure of the giving of Christ.' (Eph. 4: 7)

Simplified and purified
we become the throne of the unchangeable One,
for Unity is the very throne of the Blessed Trinity.

DAY 3
In God's presence

*We who first hoped in Christ have been destined and
appointed to live for the praise of his glory. (Eph. 1: 12)*

It is St Paul who tells us about this divine election;
St Paul who penetrates so deeply into the mystery

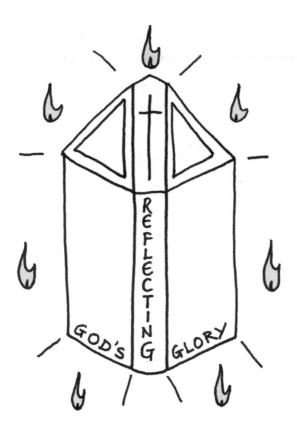

'hidden in God from all eternity'. (Eph. 3: 9)
Let us listen to him telling us that we have been chosen
before the foundation of the world to be holy and
unspotted in his sight through love. (cf Eph. 1: 4)

To fulfil my vocation of being a 'Praise of Glory' I must
keep myself in God's presence whatever happens. I must
abide always in love for 'God is Love'. (1 Jn 4: 8)
Contact with the Divinity makes us holy and unspotted,
and thus we enter into the Sabbath rest of God.

The saints in glory contemplate God
in the simplicity of God's being.
There we too shall know as we are known,
by a simple glance,
being 'transformed into his likeness
from one degree of glory to another.' (2 Cor. 3: 18)

I believe that we can give God immense joy
by imitating the blessed even now;
by living like them in the heaven of our soul,
resembling the innocence in which human beings were first
created.

God who created us in the divine likeness
wants to see the divine perfections reflected in us
as in a pure and flawless crystal.
Surely this is an extension of God's own glory;
for by gazing on God
we are lifted above self and created things
and become resplendent with
the 'light of the knowledge of the glory of God.' (2 Cor. 4: 6)

DAY 4
Faith

The city has no need of sun or moon to shine upon it,
for the glory of God is its light,
and its lamp is the Lamb. (Rev. 21: 23)

Today, St John, the disciple whom Jesus loved,
will be the one who opens for me a glimpse
into the heavenly Jerusalem, blessed city of peace.

If I want my inner city to resemble this new Jerusalem
and to shine with the light given by God,
I must first extinguish every other light,
so that the Lamb may be its only lamp.

Here the light of faith appears to me as most important.
It is faith, nothing else, that ought to enlighten me
as I go to meet the Bridegroom.

It is said of Moses that
'He endured as seeing him who is invisible,' (Heb. 11: 27)
Such should be my own attitude.
A 'Praise of Glory' wants to persevere
in her hymn of thanksgiving, whatever happens.
She wants to persevere in faith as if she saw the invisible One,
knowing and believing in the love God has for her.

'Faith is the assurance of things hoped for,

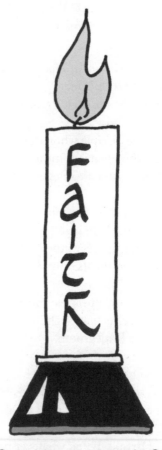

OUR LIGHT IN DARKNESS

the conviction of things not seen.' (Heb. 11: 1)
So what does it matter whether we feel anything or not,
whether we are in light or darkness,
whether we are enjoying or not enjoying life.
We should be ashamed at making distinctions like this
and turn at once to our Master,
wanting only to be united to him in love.

To us should be applied the words of St Peter:
'Without having seen him, you love him;
though you do not now see him you believe in him,
and rejoice with unutterable and exalted joy.' (1 Pet. 1: 8)

DAY 5
On the way to calvary

I saw a great multitude impossible to count...
Who are they...?
These are they who have come out of the great tribulation;
they have washed their robes and made them white in the
blood of the Lamb. Therefore they are before the throne of
God and serve him night and day in his temple; and he who
sits upon the throne will shelter them with his presence...
(Rev 7: 9-17)

All these chosen ones, palms in hand, bathed in the light
of God, have to have first passed through tribulation

and known sorrow 'great as the sea'. (Lam. 2: 13)
Before being able to behold the Lord face to face
they have shared the humiliations of Christ.
Before bearing the image of his glory
they have been conformed to the Word incarnate,
crucified by love.

Those who long to serve God day and night in his temple,
(that is, in their inmost selves, for we are God's temple),
must be resolved to take a real share
in the passion of the Master.
When we are redeemed ourselves
we, in our turn, must redeem others.
Therefore we should sing with St Paul:
'With Christ I am nailed to the cross.' (Gal. 2: 19)
and 'In my flesh I complete what is lacking
in the sufferings of Christ's afflictions
for the sake of his body, that is, the Church.' (Col. 1: 24)

The attitude of the one who walks to Calvary with Christ
is that of the queen at the right hand
of her crucified, crushed and humbled king.
He goes forth to the glory of his passion,
calm and strong, and he wants his bride to join him in the
work of redemption.

The way of sorrow she treads seems a way of blessings;
not only because it leads to Calvary,
but because she understands

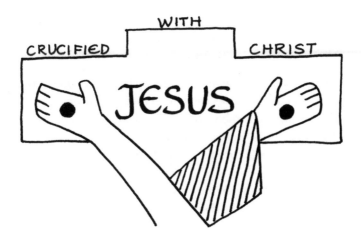

that she must pass beyond the bitterness of suffering
to find rest in it, as did her Master.

Then she is able to serve God day and night in his temple.
No outward or inward difficulties
can make her leave the holy fortress
where God has enclosed her.
She no longer hungers or thirsts for anything
except the will of the Father.
She can be led to the fountains of living water
for she looks not at the path
but only on the shepherd who guides her.
Truly, in her the Father recognises
the image of his Son, his firstborn.

DAY 6
Virgin souls

There are some on earth who already bear the name of the Lamb and of his Father written on their foreheads.
They are like the Lamb who St John calls 'faithful and true'.
They wear robes stained with blood,
the blood of their complete self-giving love.

They bear the name of the Father because he is reflected in them. They are like the strings of an instrument vibrating together with the melody of a 'new song'.

These Christians 'follow the Lamb wherever he goes', whether they travel a wide and level road, or go by thorny

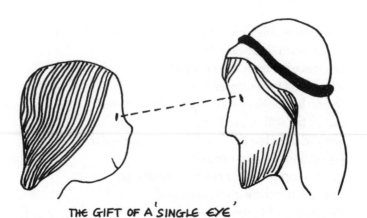

THE GIFT OF A 'SINGLE EYE'

paths among brambles. 'They are virgins.' That is, they
are free, detached from everything heavenly and earthly.
What a going out from self that implies!

We must gaze upon the Master with a 'single eye'
which makes the whole body full of light
and preserves us from sin.
A 'single eye' brings us into a spacious place
where God dwells.
There all is pure. All is holy.

O blessed death in God!
O sweet and delightful loss of self within him whom we love!
From now on we can say:
'I live, now no longer I, but Christ lives in me.
I live by faith in the Son of God who loved me
and gave himself up for me.' (Gal. 2: 20)

DAY 7
Nothing but the glory of the eternal

The heavens proclaim the glory of God. (Ps. 18: 2)

Since my soul is a heaven
where I dwell while I await the heavenly Jerusalem,
this heaven too must sing the glory of the Eternal,
and nothing but the glory of the Eternal.

God comes to me TODAY.
I must live in his light and speak of his glory.

Even my faults and ignorance can declare God's glory.
Even my sufferings can declare God's glory.
I can shine with the glory of God
when I keep my gaze fixed on him.

The psalmist sings: 'What shall I render to the Lord
for all his goodness to me?
I will lift up the cup of salvation,
and call on the name of the Lord.' (Ps. 115: 12-13)
If I take this chalice, crimsoned with my Master's blood,
and in joyful thanksgiving mingle my own blood
with that of the sacred victim,
it will be a kind of speech praising the eternal One.

If the Bridegroom finds my soul empty of everything

that is not included in his love and his glory,
then he chooses me as his bridal chamber.
He enters like a giant ready to run his course,
so that I am unable to hide from his heat.
This is the consuming fire that will ultimately transform me
into itself.

DAY 8
Holy, holy, holy is the Lord

*Night and day they never cease to sing; Holy, holy, holy, is
the Lord God Almighty, who was and is and is to come.'
They cast their crowns before the throne, singing: 'Worthy
are you our Lord and God to receive glory, honour and
power.' (Rev. 4: 8-11)*

How can I imitate the ceaseless occupation of those in
heaven, the heaven that is within me even now?
How can I maintain an attitude of constant praise and
adoration?

St Paul prays that God will grant us
to be strengthened by the Spirit,
with Christ dwelling in our hearts by faith
and ourselves being rooted and grounded in love. (cf Eph.
3: 6 -7)

HOLY · HOLY · HOLY

ADORATION! A WORD STRAIGHT FROM HEAVEN

To be rooted and grounded in love
is the condition for being a 'Praise of Glory'.
Then everything is done in love
because our gaze rests unerringly on God.
Then every action, even the most ordinary,
is a way or worshipping the Trinity.

We must plunge into the depths of our nothingness.
When we have gone as low as possible we shall find peace,
for no one can follow us when we are in our deepest depths.

Adoration! To me that is a word straight from heaven.
I would define it as an ecstasy of love;
love crushed by the beauty, the grandeur, the strength,
of the One whom we love. 'Silence is your praise.'
Yes, silence is the most perfect praise
that is sung eternally in the heart of the Trinity.

It is 'the final effort of the soul
that overflows and can speak no more.' (Lacordaire)

DAY 9
Be holy as I am holy

Be holy as I am holy. (Lev 19: 2)

Who can ask this of us?
Only the One who revealed himself to Moses,
the One in whom 'we live and move and have our being'.
(Acts 17: 28)

It seems to me that the desire for our holiness
is expressed in the very act of our creation,
when God made humans in his own image and likeness.

The Creator has always wanted to identify us with himself.
We are God's children even now,
and later we shall be totally conformed to the divine
likeness.

To be holy as God is holy.
This what the Master meant when he exhorted us to
'be perfect as your heavenly Father is perfect.' (Mt. 5: 48)
God wanted Abraham to walk before him
in like perfection.

We have indeed been chosen to walk before him
in love and purity.

To walk in holiness is to trust
under the shadow of God's wings.
There is nothing to be afraid of here.
We travel alone with the Alone who supports us.

God invites us to lose sight of self:
'My adopted daughter, look upon me.
Flow into me that I may flow into you.
Die to yourself so as to live a new life in me,
a life of holiness and perfection.'
Death is then swallowed up in victory.

TRUST

TRAVEL ... ... BENEATH GOD'S WINGS

DAY 10
The eternal present

Being perfect means that I am being asked to live
in the eternal present – God's NOW – a time of adoration.

To be the bride of Christ, the temple of the Holy Spirit,
we must have a lively faith,
and keep our eyes fixed on God alone.

We must say with the psalmist:
'I will walk with integrity of heart within my house,
I will not set before my eyes whatever is base.' (Ps. 100:2)

To be a bride is to adore God for God's sake,
wanting nothing for self.

I must try to cherish an interior stillness
by keeping myself always in silence and detachment.
If my own wants and needs, joys and sorrows,
are not totally subjected to God,
there will be inner turmoil instead of divine calm.

'Listen O daughter, give ear to my words,
forget your own people and your father's house.
The king shall greatly desire your beauty.' (Ps. 44:10-11)
But in order to listen we must forget 'our father's house'.
We must forget our own memories, hopes dreams,
all that fills up space within us.
Then we will attain the beauty of God's own unity.

DAY 11
The holy Trinity dwells in us

The Lord brought me forth into a broad place;
he delivered me because he delighted in me. (Ps. 17: 19)

The Creator, seeing silence reign in the creature
who lives recollected in deep interior solitude,
greatly desires her beauty.
Therefore, God leads her into the broad place
of his divine self.

Hosea says that the Lord 'Will lead her into solitude
and speak to her heart.' (Hos. 2: 14)
Now we have entered into that vast solitude
in which the voice of God can be heard.

'For the word of God is living and active,
sharper than any two-edged sword,
piercing to the division of soul and spirit,
of joints and marrow,
discerning the thoughts and intentions of the heart.' (Heb.
4: 12)

It is the Word himself
who will finish the divine work of creating us anew,
provided that we consent to this being done.

The persons of the Trinity dwell in the one
who loves in truth and keeps God's word.
When we realise what riches are ours for the taking,
then all the natural and supernatural joys
that might come to us from created beings, or even God,
only encourage us to enter within ourselves
and enjoy what is already ours – God.

I must leave myself always free so that I love what God loves,
and do what God would have me do.
My will, my powers of choice, must be enclosed
within the very will of God.
Then I can live freely in the eternal present.

DAY 12
By Christ I have access to the Father

The Word became flesh and dwelt amongst us. (Jn 1: 14)

God alone remains inaccessible and hidden.
We needed Jesus to descend to us, to live our life,
so that we might see what holiness is
and walk in his footsteps.

JESUS OUR aLL +

Jesus says that he sanctifies himself
so that we also may be sanctified in truth. (cf Jn 17: 19)
Christ is our hope of glory, our wisdom, our teacher of love.
Christ is our peace.
Through him we have access to the Father.
With him we are buried in Baptism;
in him we rise by faith in his resurrection.

He has made us holy by shedding his blood for us on the cross. Through him we are presented holy and spotless before the Father.

Christ wants to be my peace
so that nothing can distract me from him,
nothing can draw me away from holy recollection.
There he will give me that heavenly calm
that makes me live as though already in eternity.
By the blood of his cross he makes my inner being
a place where God can rest as in a little heaven.

Though I may fall continually,
in trustful faith I will ask him to raise me up,
knowing that he will forgive me and cleanse me.
More than that; he will strip me of all that displeases him,
all that is an obstacle to the divine action within me.
He will draw all my powers to himself and hold them
captive.

Then I shall live completely in him and will be able to say; 'I live, now no longer I, but Christ lives in me.' (Gal. 2: 20) and I shall be holy, blameless and unspotted in the Father's sight.

DAY 13
Walk in Jesus Christ

God wants to re-establish all things in Christ. (cf Eph. 1: 10)

Therefore I must walk in him, be rooted in him, built
up in him, confirmed in my faith, abounding with
thanksgiving.

When we are truly rooted in God,
the divine sap can flow freely through us
and destroy in us whatever is imperfect, trivial, or too natural.
When we are stripped of self and clothed in Christ,
we have nothing to fear from internal difficulties
or external problems.
Everything that happens only roots us more deeply
in our love for the Master.

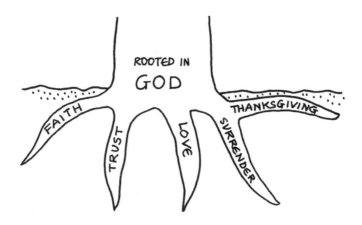

We must be confirmed in a faith
which is always alert, never slumbering,
always keeping watch under the eyes of the Master,
listening to him in faith
so that we may be filled with all the fulness of God.

Everything should then be completed with thanksgiving.
Jesus was always giving thanks
and he wants to hear the same echo within us.
The 'new song' that he wants to hear
is the song of abandonment,
by which we hand ourselves over to him
to do all he desires within us.
We must be like a lyre awaiting the divine touch,
all the strings of our being vibrating with his gifts,
and giving forth the music that is the 'praise of his glory'.

DAY 14
Knowing Christ

*I count everything as loss because of the surpassing worth of
knowing Christ Jesus my Lord. (Phil. 3: 8)*

St Paul has already given us the ground of our vocation
in that God chose us to live in his sight,
holy and unspotted.
To live in Christ is to be made conformable

SAFE IN THE HANDS OF THE FATHER

to the image of the Son of God.
Becoming like Christ we can be 'other Christs'
before the face of the Father.

On coming into the world
Jesus wanted only to do the Father's will.
'Behold I come to do your will O God.' (Heb. 10: 9)
This must be the heartbeat of the bride.
We must feed upon the will of God as did Christ the
Bridegroom.

Jesus asked that the chalice might pass from him,
yet he reiterated his desire to do the Father's will.

That must be our attitude also.
Keeping close to Jesus we learn the attributes of his heart.
By becoming like him we save others.

When we seem to fail or fall
we will learn from the silence of Jesus before his persecutors.
When we feel abandoned
we can remember his sense of abandonment on the cross.
When we feel forsaken
we will drain the chalice to the dregs
and find at the bottom a heavenly sweetness.

Thirsting for God, crying 'I thirst' with Jesus,
we will ultimately be able to sing with him
that 'It is consummated'.
Then we can surrender ourselves into the hands of the Father
walk into the kingdom of light,
and so reach perfect fulfilment.

DAY 15
Mary – 'Janua Coeli' – gate of heaven

After Jesus Christ, and infinitely far from him,
there exists a created being
who was also the great 'Praise of Glory' of the Holy Trinity.
She lived her calling to the full,
always holy, blameless and unspotted in God's sight.

WITH MARY

'His mother kept all these things in her heart.' (Lk. 1: 40,48)
Her whole history is summed up in these words.
When I read in the Gospel that Mary
went into the hill country with haste to a city of Judah
to offer loving help to her cousin ELizabeth,
I picture her to myself as she passes: beautiful, calm, majestic,
absorbed in communion with the Word dwelling within her.
Like her Son her prayer was always 'Ecce', here I am!
Who? The handmaid of the Lord, his mother.

Mary's humility was so genuine.
She was always self-forgetful, unself-conscious.
She could sing
'He who is mighty has done great things for me.
All generations will call me blessed.' (Lk. 2: 35)

The Queen of Virgins is also the Queen of Martyrs.
But the sword pierced her heart, not her body.
With Mary everything takes place within.
She has learned from her Son
how to suffer strongly and sweetly.

Mary has been chosen to be associated
in the work of redemption.
At the foot of the cross
she stands steadfast in strength and courage.
And my Master says to me: 'Behold your mother.' (Jn 19: 27)
Mary, my mother, is the one who will teach me
how to suffer for the sake of Christ's body, the Church.

She will help me hear the last outpourings of Christ's soul
which only a mother can catch.

When I have said my own 'It is consummated'
it will be Mary, 'Janua Coeli', Gate of Heaven, who will
lead me into the eternal courts.

DAY 16
In the heart of the tranquil Trinity

As a hart longs for flowing streams,
so longs my soul for thee, O God.
My soul thirsts for God, for the living God,
when shall I come and behold the face of God? (Ps. 41: 1-2)
Even the sparrow finds a home,
and the swallow a nest for herself
where she may lay her young, at thy altars,
O Lord of hosts, my King and my God. (Ps. 83: 3)

For myself, I have found my heaven here on earth
where I have already begun the life of eternity.
God is my rock, my salvation, my deliverance.
I stand firm in the Lord.

God invites me as he invited Zacchaeus 'to come down'
that the Lord may abide in my house. (cf Lk. 19: 5)
I must make haste then to descend

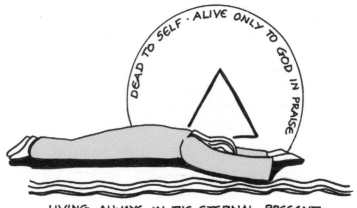

LIVING ALWAYS IN THE ETERNAL PRESENT

into the innermost depths of my being, stripped of self.
Then I can abide in the heart of the tranquil Trinity,
dying to this life and already flowing into God.

Being stripped of self
is to be resting in the immense Father,
the immense Son, the immense Spirit of holiness.

There we can live in the eternal present,
adoring God, with a gaze ever more simple and profound,
living forever in the the presence of the One we love:
a true 'Praise of Glory'.

I AM GOING TO LIGHT · LOVE · LIFE ·

POSTSCRIPT

Elizabeth was twenty six years and three months old when death came for her on November 9th, 1906, feast of the Dedication of the Lateran Basilica. She had entered Carmel on the feast of the dedication of a Church and she left it on another such feast, fulfilling her Baptismal name of 'house of God'. Her last words were: 'I am going to Light, to Love, to Life.'

Therese of Lisieux, Elizabeth's younger contemporary, had said that she would spend her heaven doing good on earth. In contrast Elizabeth said that her mission would be to help others go out of themselves, to cling to God in silence, allowing him to transform them into the image of Christ the Son. As for her, she intended to fly straight to the heart of the Trinity, there to adore God forever in silence and self-forgetfulness – a true 'Praise of Glory'.

FOR FURTHER READING

TEXTS

Alitheia Kane OCD:
(Transl)

Complete works of Elizabeth of the Trinity
Vol. I: General Introduction and Major Spiritual Writings, ICS Publications, Washington, 1984

Anne Englund Nash:
(Transl)

Complete works of Elizabeth of the Trinity
Vol. II: Letters From Carmel. ICS Publications, Washington, 1995

(Vol. III: in preparation)

LIFE, THEOLOGY AND SPIRITUALITY

Boriello, Luigi:

Spiritual Doctrine of Blessed Elizabeth of the Trinity, Alba House, New York, 1986

Germaine, Mother: *The 'Praise of Glory' – Reminiscences of Sister Elizabeth of the Trinity,* R & T, Washbourne, 1913

Mosley, Joanne: *Elizabeth of the Trinity, the unfolding of her message,*
Vol. I: In the World and in the Community
Teresian Press, 2012
Vol. II: In the Infirmary and after her Death,
Teresian Press, 2012

de Meester, Conrad (ed): *Light, Love, Life, Elizabeth of the Trinity – A Look at a Face and a Heart,* ICS Publications, Washington, 2002

Moorcroft, Jennifer: *He is My Heaven, the Life of Elizabeth of the Trinity,* ICS Publications, Washington, 2001

Murphy, Marian T. OCD: *Elizabeth of the Trinity – Always Believe in Love,* New City Press, New York, 2009

Philipon, M.M.:   *The Spiritual Doctrine of Sr Eliza-beth of the Trinity,* Mercier Press, Cork, 1947

Urs von Balthazar, Hans: *Elizabeth of Dijon,* Harvill Press, London, 1956